Table of Contents

Chapter 1 1

Chapter 2: The 5 Steps to Remember Any Name 5

Chapter 3: Putting the 5 Steps together 23

Chapter 4: The Name Test 25

Chapter 5: Name Recall Test 41

Chapter 6: Check Your Answers 57

Chapter 7: Pictures for Names from Around the World 61

I never forget a face, I just can't recall the name!

I'm not good at remembering names!

Two seconds after the handshake breaks I can't remember the name!

How many times have you said these things?

I bet lots. I wouldn't be surprised if you met someone today and right now if you thought about it you couldn't recall their name. The waiter? The bank teller? The student? The teacher? Your friend's neighbor?

Can't recall can you?

It's ok.

But there is an answer. There is a solution. And it is an important solution. It is important to remember names and faces.

Why?

Why is it important to remember names and faces?

Dale Carnegie wrote in his best selling book, 'How to Win Friends and Influence People' that :
1. Everyone's favorite subject is themselves
2. The sweetest sound to a person's ear is the sound of their own name

When you remember a name you aren't just remembering a word. You are remembering what Dale Carnegie described as their favorite subject and sweetest sound to their ear.

Think about this. You sell insurance and you are at your friend Steve's house. It is a party and your friend introduces you to his friend Brian. Six weeks later you see Brian at a baseball game.

Scenario #1

You see Brian at the game and you don't walk up to him and say hello because you can't recall the name. (Face it. You do this all the time) The odds of him purchasing insurance from you one day?

Scenario #2

You see Brian at the game and you walk up to him and say, 'Hey, I met you at Steve's house. I remember your face but sorry I can't recall your name. What was it again?' Not bad but did it right away say, 'I'm your friend!' Not really.

Scenario #3

You see Brian at the game and you walk up to him and say, 'Hey, Brian! It's great to see you again. We met at Steve's house. By the way, how is your son Matt doing and your wife Katy?' BOOM!! Does that say, 'Hey, I care and I'm your friend?' Yes it does!

It is powerful to remember names and faces. It creates an instant connection.

Zig Ziglar used to say, 'People don't care how much you know until they first know how much you care.'

When you recall a name you are showing them that you care (even more powerful than just saying it). It is a measure of respect when you recall a name. The person thinks, 'Wow, I must be special they remembered my name.'

If you are in the insurance business the odds of them purchasing from you if scenario #3 took place as opposed to scenario #1 or #2 I think you would agree are a lot higher.

But it's not just about building your business. It is about showing people that you care and building relationships.

The bad news:

It is killing your business and income that you aren't able to build relationships and remember names.

The good news:

It is easier than you think to remember names and faces. My students have learned to walk into a room and after 15 minutes can recall 20-30 names. No joke.

I'm a huge introvert but I can still do this. As a matter of fact, it gives me confidence when I met people because I have a goal or purpose in the meeting (to remember their name). So it has helped me on that level as well.

There is no magic, it doesn't require a high IQ and works no matter how terrible you think your memory is. All it requires is a little work.

When I was on the show Stan Lee's Superhumans on the History Channel I memorized the names of runners in a race and called out their names as they crossed a finish line. When I was on the National Geographic show Brain Games I memorized the names of a group as they entered a theatre and recalled the names as they exited.

I look forward to teaching you these techniques that literally people all over the world are using to remember names and build relationships.

Free $27 Name memory training videos gift.
Get it at memorizenames.com

The 5 Steps to Remember Any Name

2

What you are going to learn in this book is a system to remember names. A simple 5 step process that will enable you to recall any name or even a room full of names.

It is not route memorization or another way of saying that is it is not just saying the name 5 times over and over in the conversation. This sounds corny and everyone knows what you are doing. Stop it.

This system also is not magic. It is not something that you should just try. In other words, don't say to yourself, 'I think I will try that.'

No. Don't try this. That sounds like you are planning to fail. Instead, approach this as a system you are going to learn and implement. I hope you see the difference in mindset there.

I learned this system when I was 18 years old and no one saw anything spectacular in regards to my memory before I learned this system. However, after I learned it I have gone on to memorize 128 names in 15 minutes at the USA Memory Championship, memorize 301 names at a conference in Canada and 100 plus names at meetings more times than I can count.

With that said, it is more important that my students have been able to duplicate these same results.

In 1991 I was taught a process to remember names and I have simplified it and created 5 steps. Those 5 steps are:

1. Focus
2. File
3. Image
4. Action
5. Review

Step #1 Focus

Why do you think you don't remember names right now? Think about it. How many times have you shaken someone's hand and then 2 seconds later you don't know their name? It happens all the time to most people, but ask yourself this. Did you really remember the name and then forget it in 2 seconds? No. That's impossible. Instead, what occurred is that you never really heard the name in the first place. In other words, you were listening. You weren't paying attention. YOU WEREN'T FOCUSED!!

The first key to remember names it o FOCUS.

What this means is that the average person when they are walking up to that new person they are thinking:

'Does this person know me?

Have I seen them before?

Are the going to buy anything from me?

Do they like me?

Do I like them?

Do I still have that stain on my shirt from lunch?

Are they a customer of mine?

I need to send that email!

Will I like this person?'

All these things (or similar things) are running through your mind so fast as you meet this new person. However, the most important question is nowhere near your brain and that is why you don't remember their name.

From now on, replace all these questions that don't serve you with one question and ask it over and over as you walk towards someone you are about to meet. Train your brain when it sees a new person to ask yourself:

'What is their name?

What is their name?

What is their name?

What is their name?

What is their name?'

Ask this question over and over as you walk towards that new person. This will accomplish one very important goal and that is to FOCUS your brain.

Now, obviously you don't say this question out loud in an audible voice :)

Once your brain is focused you are then able to hear the name and eventually remember it.

A few other things can improve your ability to focus as well.

Good nutrition and exercise will improve your memory and ability to focus (even if just a little). Foods that have been known to help your brain and ability to focus are:

1. Spinach
2. Blueberries
3. Omega 3
4. Plenty of water
5. Pumpkin seeds
6. Apples

Exercise is also one of the best things that you can do for your brain and memory. It clears the cobwebs off the gears of your mind.

There are things that are bad for your brain and ability to focus as well and those include:

1. Lack of sleep
2. Excessive alcohol
3. Excessive sugar
4. Excessive salt
5. Artificial sweeteners
6. Junk food

If it's bad for your body is it going to be bad for one of the most important part of your bodies and that is your brain!

Step #2 File

The second key to remembering names is to have a file. In other words a place to store the data.

Think about your computer right now. You have a documents folder, picture folder, work folder, personal folder, movies folder and so on. But what is you didn't. What if every singe file on your computer was not in a folder but instead it was in a cluttered mess on your desk top. You would be looking at a screen with thousands of icons on your desktop and it would take you hours to find a single file!

You would never store data on your computer this way, yet we expect the human computer to remember information when it is stored on the desktop of our brains.

Instead let's place the name in a file to retrieve it later easily.

But what is a file for a name? Well, it's not going to be an actual folder but instead a unique feature on their face.

For example if you meet a person with a large nose, well…there nose becomes their file for you.

A person with a beard, their beard would be your file.

Unibrow? That becomes your file.

Pretty blue eyes? That becomes your file.

Now understand this, when I say file I simply mean a brain trigger to help you remember the person and their name. You can practice this any time even if you aren't trying to remember the names.

The next time you are at a restaurant look around and ask yourself, 'What stands out on his face? What stands out on her face?'

Eventually you will start finding patterns in the things you look for:

- Facial hair
- Thick eyebrows
- Thin eyebrows
- Pretty eyes
- Thick lips
- Thin lips
- Scars
- Moles, freckles
- Wrinkles
- Large nose
- Small nose
- Dimples in chin
- Large chin
- Big ears
- Cheek bones
- Sideburns
- Bald
- Large forehead
- Curly hair
- Thick hair
- Thin hair
- Straight teeth
- Crooked teeth
- Fat cheeks
- Dimples
- Large nostrils
- Small nostrils

- Glasses (if they wear them most of the time, i.e. not reading glasses)
- Forehead wrinkles
- Double chin

The list goes on and on because faces are unique.

You are not only observing one feature. You observe the entire face but that feature is your file or starting point to recall the name.

What do you do now when you see someone and you know you should know their name but you can't recall it? You will ask yourself, 'Oh shoot! What's their name? What's their name?'

This is one of the worst things you could do because it creates stress and stress is the worst enemy for your brain to recall the name. When I am at a conference and trying to meet and recall 100 names in an audience as I am repeating the names from stage if I don't know a name I won't stop the demo. Instead, I will skip that person and keep moving. This allows my brain to stay relaxed and then when I am done with the demo I go back to the ones who are standing.

If I stopped when I didn't know a name it might stress out my brain and then I would forget the ones that I knew.

From now on instead of trying to recall the name of a person that you have met before, instead you will ask yourself, 'What stands out to me on their face?'

In other words : What was their FILE?

Let's take a few faces as examples. What stands out to you on these faces?

Face #1

You could use many things here. Her eyebrows, nose, lips, thin eyebrows or lines coming down from her nose.

Face #2

I'd probably zoom in on her nose as her file.

Face #3

The bright red lips stand out but that may be simply because of the lipstick. So I would stay away from that. What if you see her in 3 days and she has no lipstick? For that reason I would zoom in on her cheeks.

Face #4

Her eyebrows seem to go up in an arch so that would be her file for me

Face #5

Smile is great but she may not be smiling next time you see her. So select more permanent and non mood influenced files. I would go with the eyes for sure.

Face #6

If the glasses are worn by her all day (ie not just reading glasses then they are a good file. If not I would go with the lines that come down from her nose. Some call these smile lines

Face #7

That double chin
is his file

Face #8

If you select anything but
his beard I'd be interested
in hearing what it is.

Face #9

Honestly I would use hair color here because it doesn't look like his natural color and that stands out. You might also use white teeth but there is a danger in that if he isn't smiling like this when you see him again

Face #10

Hey amigo!

I am going to use your bald head (which I will have one day too…)

So I hope you get the idea here what facial files are. The goal is to observe the face and select a distinguishing feature that you will return to later to remember the name.

Practice this overtime you see a face in person, on the tv, in print or wherever. You will get better and better at this. It is a key step in observing the face.

Step #3 Image

Whatever you want to remember it needs to be a picture.

Your mind thinks in pictures. Don't believe me? When you dream are you seeing pictures or are you reading words?

You are seeing pictures.

How many times have you said, 'I am so good with faces. I never forget a face. I just can't think of your name?' - Big deal by the way... my DOG remembers your face :) ha

The REASON you remember a face and not a name is you SAW the face. You never SAW the name.

You mind thinks in pictures. Period.

Try this.

I want to introduce you to my friends: Lisa, Al, Steve, Brian and Tammy.

Now

We are going to play a game here

It will be fun.

And interesting.

And...

Important.

Now…

Do NOT

Do NOT

Do NOT

Do NOT cheat.

But without reading their names again, Can you tell me who they were? Their names I just gave you?

Mabye but not easily.

Why? They weren't pictures they were just words.

Imagine this scenario…

You are looking at the Mona Lisa and an owl flies in the room. You put it on the stove to cook the owl. The owl's brain pops out and you put the brain in your tummy.

So try this.

We are going to play a game here.

It will be fun.

And interesting.

I want you to do something.

Tell me the story I just told you. What was the story?

(pause here to remember the story)

I bet you were able to remember this story easier than remembering the names Lisa, Al, Steve, Brian and Tammy. Why?

Because the story is a picture and names are not. By the way. These pictures are my pictures for the names I just gave you.

Lisa = Mona Lisa

Al = owl

Steve = stove

Brian = brain

Tammy = tummy

These are the kinds of pictures you will need to remember names.

How do you turn a name into a picture? Here are my rules.

10 Commandments of Turning Names into Pictures

1. Don't use people to remember other people. For example, if the name is Steve don't say, 'Oh that's easy my cousin is named Steve.' Well the next time you see him you might get confused. Was it your cousin Steve or your cousin Brian?

2. I'm going to break rule #1 right now. If the name is Elvis, Madonna or Adolf. Yes…I will use other people. But those are the exception.

3. Think of a concrete noun that is clear and simple. Steve = stove, Brian = brain, Matt = door mat

4. Break the name down by syllable. Christopher = Chris/to/fer = Chris/toe/fur = Cross with a toe and fur (I simplify it often to just a cross with fur)

5. Different variations of a name MUST have different pictures. For example:
    Al = owl
    Albert = burnt owl
    Chris = cross
    Christopher = cross with fur
    Judy = chew tea
    Judith = chew this
    Christine = christening (baby baptism)
    Christy = cross with tea

Kristin = kiss a ton

6. Don't over think it. Go with the first thing that pops in to your mind. It doesn't have to make sense to anyone else but you. For example the name Jessica I use a dresser (like furniture). That probably doesn't make sense to you but it doesn't have to

7. Use the same picture EVERY time. For example, if you determine that you picture for Paul is a basketball then use that for EVERY Paul. Every Paul for the rest of your life will be a basketball. This is a very important step. If you start switching the pictures for names up this will be too confusing and too much work.

8. Every time you meet a person from now on if you don't have a picture for their name ask yourself, 'What would a picture for this name be?'

9. If in a conversation you find yourself not listening to the person but instead trying to think of a picture for their name then STOP turning their name into a picture and focus on the person and conversation and return to the process after you leave that person.

10. You don't need different pictures for different spellings (ie Jeffrey and Jeffery) unless you feel writing this name is important. If so, create rules for yourself. Jeffrey = chef reading (reading to remind you it ends in RE and not ER). Jeffery = chef in the ER (ER to remind you it ends in ER and not RE)

Once you have a picture for the name you will visualize or imagine this picture on the face on the unique or distinctive facial feature.

So if the outstanding facial feature is the nose and the name is Steve you imagine that Stove on the nose.

Some examples of my pictures for names would be:

Steve = stove
Brian = brain
Karen = carrot

Frank = frankfurter
Dave = cave
David = divot
Paul = basketball
Wayne = rain
Vince = fence
Michelle = missile
Wendy = wind
Monica = harmonica
Lisa = Mona Lisa

Step #4 Action

Your mind remember action and emotion.

Think about it.

Where were you on September 11th? If you are old enough to remember you recall vividly.

I was only 13 when the Space Shuttle exploded in 1986 but I remember telling my dad and his reaction to what I told him I was watching on television. I didn't understand the magnitude of what I was watching and probably wouldn't haven't remembered that day if it was not for his reaction.

Have you ever been in a car accident? If so:
- Who was driving?
- What area of town did it occur?
- Day or night?
- Who was in the car?
- Did your car wreck into another car or did they crash into you?
- How many years ago was this?

I bet if it was 20 years ago you still recall all the details.

I also bet that you can't tell me everywhere you drove last week as quickly and easily. Why?

Action and emotion.

These things will cement something into your memory long term.

So in regards to remembering names and faces this means if the name is Steve and you see a stove. You don't just see a stove but it needs to be cooking something. Cooking it so hot the person turns red or even catches on fire. You have to magnify the action and emotion in order to recall the name.

If you don't, then you won't.

Passive pictures don't work.

If the name is Lisa and you imagine the Mona Lisa in her eyes that may or may not work because it is kind of passive. But if you imagine DaVinci himself is painting a picture in her eyes and you see the brush, etc then you will recall this more likely.

Action and emotion with vivid pictures are the key to long term memory.

Step #5 Review

In order to put something into long term memory you must review.

If you visualize a stove coming out of Steve's ears or a brain oozing out of Brian's eyes that's great. But if you don't review you won't recall Steve or Brian's names two weeks later.

The secret to long term memory is creating vivid ACTION and EMOTION but it is also reviewing these images.

This is what I would suggest:

- When you have first met someone and are leaving ask yourself, 'What was their file? What was their name? What is the picture for this name?' and see the image with tons of action and emotion on their feature. This is how you review.
- At the end of the day repeat this process by asking, 'Who did I meet today?'

- When getting ready in the morning, driving to work, taking a shower or standing in lines use this time to review who you met the day before, week before, month before
- When you see a restaurant, hotel, house, bar or room where you met someone before ask yourself, 'Who did I meet at that restaurant (or other location)?' Use locations where you have met people as brain triggers to review the people you have met there.
- You may want to keep a name journal where you record names when you meet people. You might write things such as:

  - Steve, big ears, about 35 years old, tall
  - Lisa, pretty eyes, about 27 years old, blonde
  - Karen, small nose, about 40 yrs old, glasses

- In your name journal you will write down their distinguishing feature along with their name and other physical facts. Develop the habit of looking through this journal once a week and visualizing the faces

Free $27 Name memory training videos gift.
Get it at memorizenames.com

Putting the 5 Steps Together

Let's run through the steps very quickly.

1. Focus
2. File
3. Image
4. Action
5. Review

Using the 5 steps, you walk into a meeting and you are walking towards this woman.

1. As you walk towards her you ask yourself the question, 'What's her name? What's her name?' This focuses your memory to hear her name.

2. You observe her face and use the facial feature that jumps out at you right away. Let's use her eyebrows here (but you could certainly select anything that stands out for you)

3. Her name is Karen. The image for Karen is carrots. So imagine her eyebrows are made out of carrots.

4. Tie action and emotion to this. Imagine her eyebrows are crunchy carrots and you are eating the eyebrows. Taste the carrots if you can imagine that.

5. Review

This is how you put the 5 steps together.

So let's create a memory test.

I'm going to give you 30 pictures and I want you to take 15 minutes (for fun time yourself and see if you can do it faster). Then go through the names and faces and memorize the names. I will give you the name and my suggested picture for the name as well as my suggested file for the face. With that said, this is all about creating what works for YOU! So feel free to use something different that works best for you.

Free $27 Name memory training videos gift.
Get it at memorizenames.com

The Name Test

Set a timer and give yourself 15 minutes. 30 names and faces. (by the way, after you complete this www.memorise.org has a game that you can play to get good at names and faces)

Here we go!!

1.

Name: Lisa

Image: Mona Lisa

File: Nose

Action: She is using her nose to paint the Mona Lisa

2.

<u>Name:</u> Kelly

<u>Image:</u> key

<u>File:</u> cheeks

<u>Action:</u> You are putting a key in her cheeks and opening the door

3.

<u>Name:</u> Michelle

<u>Image:</u> missile

<u>File:</u> Eyebrows

<u>Action:</u> Her eyebrows are shooting out missiles or you are shooting her eyebrows with missiles.

4.

Name: Jane

Image: chain

File: eyes

Action: Imagine you are pulling a chain out of her eyes.

5.

Name: Lacy

Image: lace

File: glasses

Action: Imagine her glasses are trimmed with lace. These are really fancy lace glasses

6.

Name: Bill

Image: dollar bill

File: chin

Action: Dollar bills are flying out of his chin. Or you are sticking dollar bills in to his chin

7.

Name: Frank

Image: frankfurter (hot dog)

File: beard

Action: He is pulling frankfurters out of his beard and EATING THEM!!

8.

Name: Brian

Image: brain

File: hair (because of color)

Action: Imagine that his brain is oozing out of his hair and that is why it is that color

9.

Name: Wayne

Image: rain

File: bald head

Action: It's raining down on his bald head. Imagine the drops of water bouncing off his head!

10.

Name: Jenny

Image: spinning jenny (type of machine that spun cotton invented 1764)

File: eyebrows

Action: Imagine a spinning jenny machine is spinning cotton out of her eyebrows. The more you look at her the thicker her eyebrows of cotton get because of the spinning jenny

11.

Name: Wendi

Image: wind

File: Eyes

Action: The wind coming out of her eyes is blowing you over. Feel the breeze!

12.

Name: Vince

Image: fence

File: long nose

Action: Imagine a fence built along his long nose.

13.

Name: Dale

Image: chipmunk (Chip & Dale) or a Dell computer

File:hair

Action: chipmunks are running in and out of his hair

14.

Name: Claudia

Image: clouds

File: eyes

Action: Imagine her eyes are soft clouds and you are floating and relaxing in the clouds

15.

Name: Mark

Image: marker

File: hair (lower part of hair that wings out in the back)

Action: Imagine you are coloring his hair in the back with a black marker. All of his hair has been drawn in with a marker by you

16.

Name: Eva

Image: Evening (sunset)

File: lips

Action: She is kissing the sunset or you see the sunset in her lips

17.

Name: Matt

Image: door mat

File: Adam's apple

Action: You are wiping your feet on his Adam's apple that is actually a door mat

18.

<u>Name:</u> Sheila

<u>Image:</u> sheet

<u>File:</u> It's subtle but she has a gap in front teeth

<u>Action:</u> A bed sheet is being worked through that gap in her teeth. Or maybe you imagine that her teeth are beds and you put the sheet on the teeth

19.

<u>Name:</u> Brandy

<u>Image:</u> brandy (the drink)

<u>File:</u> curly hair

<u>Action:</u> Brandy is pouring down the curls of her hair. The brandy is making her hair curly and her curls taste like brandy

20.

Name: Jack

Image: car jack

File: nose

Action: You are jacking up his nose with a car jack. Imagine the grease is everywhere and you are lifting his nostrils up with the jack

21.

Name: Chris

Image: cross

File: pale skin

Action: cross sticking out of his pale skin

22.

Name: Kristin

Image: kissing a ton

File: eyes

Action: You are in love with her e[yes]
TON!

23.

Name: Tim

Image: tin (can)

File: beard

Action: His beard is
a tin can. Imagine
touching the tin can
and hearing the sound
it makes when hit

24.

Name: Kim

Image: swim

File: chin

Action: A girl is swimming from her chin all the way up her face in to her hair and around in her mouth back to the chin.

25.

Name: Paul

Image: ball

File: side burns

Action: Imagine bouncing a ball on his side burns

26.

Name: Sally

Image: salad

File: long neck

Action: Eating a salad off her neck!!

27.

Name: Dan

Image: pan

File: ears

Action: You are cooking in a pan over his ears! Imagine his ears are huge cooking pans!

28.

Name: Kailey

Image: K in leaves

File: hair

Action: Her hair is full of leaves and falling into the leaves is a huge letter K

29.

Name: Derek

Image: oil derrick

File: eyes

Action: Oil is GUSH-ING out of his eyes and you are now RICH!!!

30.

Name: Jim

Image: gym

File: hair (duh!)

Action: Imagine his hair is one big dumbbell and you are bench pressing it at the gym. Lifting that hair getting a GREAT workout at the gym!

Okay, so how was that? You just met 30 new people!!

I would recommend if you have time to go back real fast for a review once or twice to lock them in before you go to the next chapter and see how many you can recall. Remember the more action and emotion the better.

Make these images vivid and full of action and emotion.

The next chapter will be the test.

Free $27 Name memory training videos gift.
Get it at memorizenames.com

Name Recall Test

Set a timer and give yourself 15 minutes. 30 names and faces. (by the way, after you complete this www.memorise.org has a game that you can play to get good at names and faces)

INSTRUCTIONS: Number 1-30 and write down the answers. We will check your answers in the next chapter.

Here we go!!

1.

Name: ?

2.

<u>Name:</u> ?

3.

<u>Name:</u> ?

4.

Name: ?

5.

Name: ?

6.

Name: ?

7.

Name: ?

8.

<u>Name:</u> ?

9.

<u>Name:</u> ?

10.

<u>Name:</u> ?

11.

<u>Name:</u> ?

12.

Name: ?

13.

Name: ?

14.

<u>Name:</u> ?

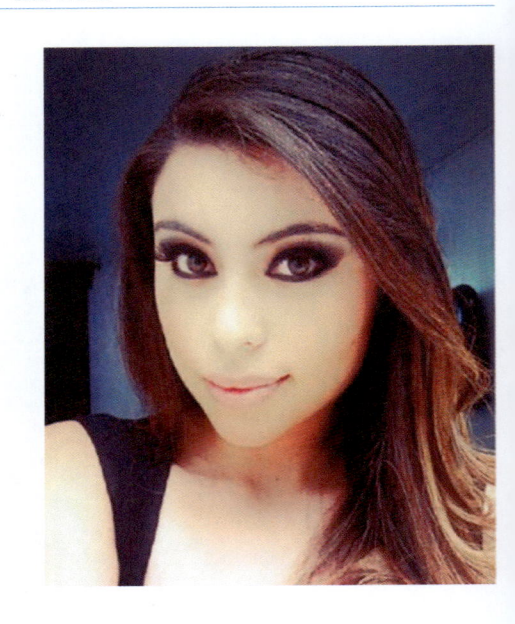

15.

<u>Name:</u> ?

16.

Name: ?

17.

Name: ?

18.

<u>Name:</u> ?

19.

<u>Name:</u> ?

20.

<u>Name:</u> ?

21.

<u>Name:</u> ?

22.

<u>Name:</u> ?

23.

<u>Name:</u> ?

24.

Name: ?

25.

Name: ?

26.

<u>Name:</u> ?

27.

<u>Name:</u> ?

28.

Name: ?

29.

Name: ?

30.

Name: ?

So how do you think you did? Make sure you wrote down your answers and in the next chapter we will check your answers!!

Check Your Answers

See how you did!!

1. Lisa
2. Kelly
3. Michelle
4. Jane
5. Lacy
6. Bill
7. Frank
8. Brian
9. Wayne
10. Jenny
11. Wendi
12. Vince
13. Dale
14. Claudia
15. Mark
16. Eva
17. Matt
18. Sheila
19. Brandy
20. Jack
21. Chris
22. Kristin
23. Tim
24. Kim
25. Paul
26. Sally
27. Dan
28. Kailey
29. Derek
30. Jim

How did you do?

If you got all 30 FANTASTIC!!! I will see you at the next World Memory Championship!

25 or more is really great!

20 or more is also very good.

If you missed any ask yourself why. Did you know your file? Was your action vivid enough? Probably not. You will find that if you miss items it will be because your action and emotion isn't vivid enough. You didn't actually see it. You simply thought it and didn't see it.

Remember at the start of this book we said you will remember faces and not names because you saw the face but you never saw the name. The same remains true here. If you are simply saying the picture but not really doing your best to imagine it then you won't remember it.

I do want to be clear also. A friend recently asked me, 'Ron, but I have trouble seeing images. I can't do this.'

YES YOU CAN!!!

Do you dream? Most likely yes. When you do are you seeing pictures? Yes.

Have you ever day dreamed? Yes. When you do you are seeing pictures.

The expectation isn't that you see a clear, full color 3D image. I'm not. It's more of a hazy impression. So be sure that your expectations are clear on what you are supposed to be 'seeing'.

Let's review:

1. Focus - Ask yourself, 'What's their name?' As you walk to the person.
2. File - Select an outstanding feature on their face
3. Image - Create an image for their name
4. Action - See that image on their file with action and emotion
5. Review - At the end of each day ask yourself, 'Who did I meet today?'

Why go through the trouble of remembering names?

Zig Ziglar said, 'People don't care how much you know until they first know how much you care.'

Show people that you care by remembering their name. It builds relationships and friendships.

Pictures for Names from Around the World

7

USA Female Names

Abby – A Bee

Abigail – A bee in a pail

Adell – A Bell

Alice – Lice

Allison – Lice in the sun

Amy – Aiming

Angie – Ants drinking tea

Ann – Ant

Anita – kneading

Annette – A net

Annie – Orphan Annie

April – A pill

Ashley – Ashes

Audrey – Laundry

Barbara – barbed wire

Beatrice – beat rice

Becky – horse bucking

Belinda – Bee in a window (winda)

Bernadette – burn a net

Beth – bath

Betty – betting

Beverly – bed of leaves

Billie – billy goat

Bobbie – fishing bobber

Bonnie – Bonnet

Brenda – bent window (winda)

Bridget – Bridges

Camille – camel

Candice – can of dice

Candy – candy

Carla – car with lace

Carmen – car and man

Carol – Christmas carol

Celeste – stars

Charlotte – spider web	Elaine – air plane
Cheryl – chair that is ill	Eleanor – plane landing on door
Chloe – clover	Elise – A lease
Chris – cross	Elizabeth – lizard breath
Chrissy – cross in the sea	Ellen – island
Christine – Christmas tree	Ellie – belly
Cicely – sis being silly	Emily – family
Cindy – cinnamon candy	Erica – ear
Clara – clarinet	Eve – Christmas Eve
Claudia – cloud	Evelyn – violin
Colleen – calling	Faith – church
Connie – convict	Felicia – fleece
Crystal – crystal vase	Florence – floor dance
Daphne – dolphin	Frances – Eiffel Tower
Darlene – door with beans	Gabrielle – Gabby (talking) bell
Dawn – dawn	Gail – gale force wind
Debbie – dead bee	Georgia – gorge
Deborah – dead boar	Gina – blue jeans
Denise – disease	Ginger – ginger bread man
Diana – dying ants	Ginny – bottle of gin on knees
Dixie – Confederate flag	Glenda – blender
Donna – Donald Duck	Gloria – Old Glory
Doris – doors	Grace – saying a prayer
Dorothy – tornado (Wizard of Oz)	Hannah – hand
Dottie – dots shaped like 'E'	Harriet – lariat
Edna – head saying 'ahh'	Hattie – hat with an 'E'
Eileen – eye leaning	Heather – feather

Heidi – someone hiding	June – june bug
Helen – light (what Helen means)	Karen – carrot
Holly – boughs of holly	Kate – gate
Hope – rope, soap	Katherine – cat that runs
Irene – eye ring	Kathleen – cat that leans
Iris – a wrist	Kathy – cat
Jackie – car jack	Katie – kite
Jacqueline – lint on a jack	Kay – key
Jamie – chain on your knee	Kim – swim
Jan – jam	Kirsten – skirt with a stem
Janet – jam in a net	Laura – laurels
Janice – jeans in a noose	Laurie – lowering an 'E'
Jeanette – jeans in a net	Leslie – less than sign '<'
Jeanie – genie	Lillian – lily with ants on it
Jennifer – chin fur	Lily – lily
Jenny – chinny	Linda – window (winda)
Jessica – vest with cuffs	Lisa – Mona Lisa
Jill – pill	Lois – lost 'S'
Jo – sloppy joe hamburger	Loretta – lower it
Joan – Joan of Arc	Lorraine – low rain
Joanne – sloppy joe w/ ants	Louise – low easel
Joy – Joy dishwashing liquid	Lucille – loose sail
Joyce – juice	Lucinda – loose cinder
Juanita – one knee	Lucy – I Love Lucy
Judith – blue desk	Lynn – lint
Judy – chewing tea	Madeline – mad at lint
Julie – jewelry	Mandy – mandolin

Marcy – marching	Olive – olives
Margaret – market	Olivia – oh liver!
Marge – barge	Pam – spam
Maria – sangria wine	Pamela – paneling
Marian – mare with ants	Pat – act of patting
Marie – mare with an 'E'	Patricia – pats of butter
Marilyn – marry lint	Patty – hamburger patty
Marjorie – my jury	Paula – ball with an 'A'
Marsha – marsh mellow	Pauline – pole that leans
Martha – vineyard	Peg – peg
Mary – merry go round	Penny – penny (coin)
Marry Ellen – marry a melon	Phyllis – philly
Melanie – melon on your knee	Priscilla – pass the Jello
Melissa – molasses	Rachel – ray shining on a shell
Meredith – mare in a dish	Ramona – ram moaning
Miriam – mirror ham	Rebecca – reach for the deck
Mitzi – mitt that can see	Renee – raining A's
Mona – moaning	Roberta – robot
Monica – harmonica	Robin – bird
Nan – nun	Rochelle – row of shells
Nancy – nun eating seeds	Rosa – rose ah!
Natalie – gnats	Rosalie – rose on your knee
Nellie – kneeling	Rosalyn – rosin (bag)
Nicole – Nickel	Rose – rose
Nora – snore ah!	Roxanne – rocks in hand
Noreen – no rain	Ruth – Baby Ruth candy bar
Norma – normal	Sadie – saddle

Sally – salad	Sue – suit
Samantha – saw a man	Sue Ann – suit with ants
Sandra – sander	Susan – lazy Suzan
Sandy – Sand	Susannah – snoozing
Sarah – Sarah Lee cup cakes	Tammy – tummy
Sasha – sash	Teresa – tree saw
Sherry – bottle of sherry	Terry – terry cloth
Sharon – sharing	Tess – test
Sheila – shield	Vanessa – van wearing a dress
Sheryl – chair that is ill	Vicky – Vick's cough drops
Shirley – shirt sleeves	Victoria – victory
Sidney – sit on a knee	Vivian – we win
Sylvia – silver ware	Wanda – wand
Sonia – Sony Walkman	Windy – wind
Sophia – sew a bee	Yvette – Corvette
Stacy – stay seated	Yvonne – heave on
Stephanie – step on knees	Zoe – sew an 'E'

USA Male Names

Aaron – air gun

Abe – ape

Adam – a dam

Al – owl

Alan – alan wrench

Albert – burnt owl

Alex – owl that licks

Alexander – leg sander

Alfred – owl fried

Alonzo – bonzo (clown)

Alvin – owl wins

Andrew – ants drew

Andy – ants drinking tea

Angelo – angel eating jello

Anthony – ants in a tree

Archie – archery

Armand – arm band

Arnold – arm hold

Art – art work

Arthur – author

Austin – cowboy boot (Texas)

Barney – barn

Barry – berry

Bart – dart

Ben – bench

Benny – bending

Benjamin – bend a man

Bernard – St Bernard

Bernie – burn a knee

Bert – bird

Bill – duck's bill

Bob – bobsled

Bobby – bobby pin

Brad – bread

Bradford – bread in a Ford

Bradley – bread with leaves

Brandon – branded

Brian – brain

Brock – rock with a 'B'

Bruce – bruise

Bud – rose bud

Ceasar – Julius Ceasar

Cameron – camera

Carl – curl

Carlos – car that is lost

Carter – charter a boat

Cary – carry

Cecil – seal

Cedric – red brick

Chad – chaps

Charles – charcoal

Charlie – charred leaves

Chester – chest of drawers

Chet – Jet

Chris – cross

Christian – Christ

Christopher – kiss furr

Chuck – chalk

Clark – clock

Claude – cloud

Clayton – ton of clay

Cliff – cliff

Clifford – Ford going off cliff

Clint – lint

Clinton – ton of lint

Clyde – Clydesdale horse

Cole – coal

Colin – calling

Conrad – con(vict) rat

Corey – apple core

Craig – crack

Curt – curtain

Dan – dam

Daniel – van yells

Darren – da rent

Darryl – barrel

Dave – cave

David – divot

Dennis – dentist

Derek – oil derrick

Dick – deck

Dirk – dirt

Dominick – dominoes

Don – dawn

Donald – Donald Duck

Doug – dig

Douglas – dug a glass

Drew – drew

Duane – drain

Dunking – dunking

Dusty – dusting

Dwight – white 'D'

Earl – pearl

Ed – head

Eddie – eddy

Edgar – head gear

Edmund – head mount

Edward – head ward

Edwin – head wind

Eli – eel eye

Emmanuel – a manual

Eric – ear ache

Ernie – ear and knee

Erwin – ear & wind

Ethan – eating

Evan – oven

Everette – sever it

Felix – feel it

Fletcher – fetcher

Floyd – flood

Frank – frankfurter

Fred – fried egg

Freddy – frayed 'E'

Frederick – frayed brick

Garrett – chair it

Gary – garage

Geoffrey – chef in a tree

George – gorge

Gerald – chair that is old

Gil – fish gil

Gilbert – burnt fish gils

Graham – graham crackers

Grant – granite (rock)

Greg – keg

Gus – gust of wind

Hal – hail

Hank – hankerchief

Hans – hands

Harold – hair that is old

Harry – hair

Hector – heckler

Herb – herb

Herbert – herb & bird

Howard – coward

Hugh – ewe

Irv – nerve

Irving – swerving

Isaac – eye sack

Ivan – eye on van

Jack – car jack

Jacob – Jacob's ladder

Jake – shade

James – chains

Jason – jaybird in the sun

Jay – jaybird

Jeff – chef

Jeffrey – chef in a tree

Jeremy – chair on me

Jerome – chair roam

Jerry – cherry

Jess – chest

Jim – gym

Joe – sloppy Joe hamburger

Joel – jewel

Joey – kangaroo

John – toilet

Jonah – whale

Jonathan – toilet that is thin

Jordan – jaw of tin

Jose – hose

Joshua – shower	Mack – Mack Truck
Juan – wand	Manny – man with an 'E'
Jud – jug	Mark – marker
Julio – jewel that is low	Marshall – law enforcement
Justin – justice	Martin – Martian
Keith – keys	Marvin – carving
Ken – can	Mason – mason jar
Kenneth – can on a net	Matt – door matt
Kent – tent	Matthew – matt in a pew
Kevin – cave in	Maurice – more rice
Kirk – kick	Max – mix
Kyle – tile	Maxwell – mix well
Lance – Sir Lancelot	Mel – melon
Larry – lariat	Melvin – melt van
Lawrence – law for ants	Michael – bicycle
Lee – leaves	Mickey – Mickey Mouse
Len – lens	Mike – microphone
Leo – lion	Miles – miles
Leon – lean on	Mitch – mitt
Leroy – leaves on a toy	Morris – Morris The Cat
Les – less than sign '<'	Morgan – organ
Lionel – Lionel train	Nathan – gnat in your head
Lou – blue (color)	Ned – bed
Lucas – low kiss	Neal – nail
Luke – luke warm water	Nick – nickel
Luther – roofer with an 'L'	Noah – no air
Lyle – aisle	Noel – Christmas Noel

Norman – Norseman	Robert – robot
Oliver – olive	Rod – rod
Oscar – Academy award	Roderick – rod in a brick
Otis – Otis elevator	Rodney – rod in knee
Owen – rowing	Roger – rod in chair
Pat – pat something	Roland – rolling
Patrick – St Patrick	Ron – rum
Paul – ball	Ronald – Ronald McDonald
Pedro – paid to row	Ronnie – running
Pete – Pete Moss	Ross – boss
Peter – Peter cottontail	Roy – Roy Rogers
Phil – fill up	Russ – rusts
Pierre – pier	Russell – rustle
Preston – pressing a ton	Sam – Uncle Sam
Quincy – wind and sea	Sammy – Uncle Sam on knee
Ralph – raft	Samuel – Uncle Sam on mule
Randall – ram and doll	Sandy – sand
Randolph – ram and dolphin	Scott – Scott paper towels
Randy – bottle of brandy	Shawn – yawn
Ray – ray of light	Seymour – see more
Raymond – ray on a mound	Sheldon – shielding
Rex – wrecks	Sherman – German shepard
Richard – wrench in a yard	Sid – sit
Richie – dollar sign	Stan – stand
Rick – brick	Steve – stove
Rob – robber	Stewart – steward
Robbie – robe	Stu – stew

Tad – tadpole	Tyrone – tie rowing
Teddy – teddy bear	Tyler – tire
Terry – tearing an 'E'	Van – van
Tex – Texas	Vince – fence
Theodore – see a door	Vern – fern
Thomas – thermos	Vernon – furry nun
Tim – tin can	Vic – Vick's cough drop
Timothy – tin of tea	Vincent – mint fence
Toby – toe and bee	Wade – wade in pool
Todd – toad	Wallace – walrus
Tom – tom cat	Walt – waltz
Tommy – Tommy gun	Walter – wallpaper
Tony – Tony the Tiger	Ward – ward
Tracy – tracing an 'E'	Warren – warden
Ty – tie	Wayne – rain

Top 100 USA Common Last Names

Smith – Blacksmith iron

Johnson – Toilet (John) in the sun

Williams – Will and yams

Brown – Brown color

Jones – "Jonesing"

Miller – Saw mill

Davis – Day vision

Garcia – Car seed

Rodriguez – Rod read guess

Wilson – Wilson volleyball

Martinez – Martinis

Anderson – Ants in the sun

Taylor – Suit tailor

Thomas – Thermos

Hernandez – Hurt hands

Moore – Moore a ship

Martin – Martian

Jackson – Jacks in the sun

Thompson – Thumbs on

White – Color white

Lopez – Low Pez (candy)

Lee – Leaves

Gonzalez – Gone S

Harris – Harry S

Clark – Clark Forklift

Lewis – Loose S

Robinson – Robing the sun

Walker – Walker (for patient or baby)

Perez – P rests

Hall – Hall

Young – Baby

Allen – Allen wrench

Sanchez – Sandwhich

Wright – Write

King – King crown

Scott – Scott paper towels

Green – Color green

Baker – Baker

Adams – Adam's apple

Nelson – Full nelson wrestling move

Hill – Hill

Ramirez – Ram an S

Campbell – Campbell soup

Mitchell – Missile

Roberts – Robots

Carter – Car tear

Phillips – Phillips screwdriver

Evans – Ovens

Turner – Turning

Torres – Tore an S

Parker – Parking

Collins – Calling

Edwards – Head warden

Stewart – Stew art

Flores – Flowers

Morris – Morris the Cat

Nguyen – Win

Murphy – Smurph

Rivera – River

Cook – Cook

Rogers – Rod in a chair

Morgan – Organ

Peterson – Peter Rabbit in the sun

Cooper – Barrel

Reed – Read

Bailey – Bail hay

Bell – Bell

Gomez – Go mess

Kelly – Key

Howard – Indian (How is hello)

Ward – Warden

Cox – Cocks

Diaz – Day S

Richardson – Wrench in the sun

Wood – Wood

Watson – Lightbulb (Watts)

Brooks – Water brook

Bennett – Bend a net

Gray – Gray color

James – Chains

Reyes – Rays

Cruz – Cruise ship

Hughes – Hue

Price – Price tag

Myers – My R's

Long – Something long

Foster – Take care of

Sanders – Sander

Ross – Rust

Morales – More L's and S's

Powell – Punch (POW!)

Sullivan – Sold the van

Russell – Rusty L

Ortiz – Oar tees

Jenkins – Chin can

Gutierrez – Good tears

Perry – Pear

Butler – Butler

Barnes – Barns

Fisher – Fisherman

Top 100 African Female Names

Sarah – Sahara desert

Yasmine – Jazz men

Grace – Pray (say grace)

Mariam – Marry an M

Maria – Mar (sea) and air

Linda – Window (winda)

Salma – Salmon

Inès – Eye nest

Sara – Sahara desert

Marie – Marie Antoinette (Guillotine)

Esther – A star

Aicha – Acai berry

Amina – Amino acid

Rose – Rose

Stephanie – Step on knees

Anais – A niece

Melissa – Molasses

Awa – A war

Audrey – Odd drawing

Julie – Jewelry

Sandra – Sander

Patricia – Pat rice

Aya – Eye

Florence – Florence Italy (David statue)

Vanessa – Van full of S's

Alice – Lice

Pauline – Ball lean

Anna – Ant on an A

Irene – Eye ring

Jessica – Chest of drawers

Imane – Eye mane

Samira – Samurai

Christelle – Crystal

Laura – Lowering an A

Sonia – Saw ya

Oceane – Ocean

Fatima – Fat ma

Ruth – Babe Ruth

Beatrice – Bee in trees

Lydia – Lid in air

Olivia – Olives

Aminata – Men otter

Mary – Merry Go Round

Carine – Carrying

Laetitia – Lay tissue

Cynthia – Cinnamon teeth

Nicole – Nickels

Nour – Hour(glass)

Léa – Leaves

Emma – Hem (of pants)

Lina – Line

Sophie – Soak feet

Eva – Evening (sunset)

Diane – Dying ants

Nadia – Knodding

Lisa – Mona Lisa

Maeva – Maven (NASA spacecraft)

Sharon – Sharing

Leila – Lay low

Elizabeth – Lizard breath

Flora – Flower

Jennifer – Chin fur

Edith – Eat this

Kenza – Ken doll sawed

Justine – Lady Justice

Sofia – Soak feet

Nadège – Nut edge

Estelle – Is still

Natacha – Knot tossing

Faith – Face

Oumaima – Oh Miami

Sylvie – Silver

Meriem – Marry them

Joyce – Joy (happy) ice

Larissa – La wrist

Sabrina – Submarine

Hiba – He bear

Michelle – Missile

Sophia – Soak feet

Rita – Margarita

Sandrine – Sand rind (fruit skin)

Rachel – Ray on shell

Nina – Christopher Columbus ship

Aurélie – A rally

Prisca – Princess ill

Doris – Door S

Aida – Band Aid

Chloe – Closing

Emilie – Hem (of pants) with leaves

Abigail – Ape

Christina – Christening an A

Wendy – Windy

Elodie – Loading

Anne – Ants

Mimi – My my (as if holding in arms)

Rim – Rim (wheel)

Lynda – Window (winda)

Farah – Far off

Catherine – Cat and hen

Nancy – Nun eating seeds

Top 100 African Male Names

Emmanuel – A manual

Mohamed – Mohammed Ali

Daniel – Van yell

Eric – Earache

David – Divot

Samuel – Uncle Sam on mule

Joseph – Cup of Joe sip

Ibrahim – E bra on him

Richard – Wrench in yard

Patrick – St Patrick

Christian – Christian cross

Isaac – Eye sack

Michael – Microhone yell

Francis – Eiffel Tower (France)

Adama – A dam A

Abdoulaye – Abs dueling for an A

Jean – Blue jeans

John – Toilet

Prince – Prince

Ousmane – Os on horses mane

Joel – Billy Joel

Paul – Ball

Souleymane – Soul of a horses mane

James – Chains

Alex – Owl that licks

Ahmed – A mitt

Franck – Frankfurter

Charles – Charcoal

Moussa – Moose

Yves – Heaves

Fabrice – Fabulous rice

Ibrahima – Zebra that's a him

Kevin – Cave in

Junior – June bug

Serge – Power surge

Benjamin – Been jamming

Thomas – Thermos

Oumar – O's in the mar (Spanish for sea)

Ali – All leaves

Rodrigue – Rod reading guess

Ismaël – Is mail?

Olivier – Olive

Herve – Her V

Mamadou – Mama dew

Pascal – Pass cow

François – Eiffel Tower (France) saw

Martin – Martian

Karim – Cream

Denis – Dentist

George – Gorge

Robert – Robot

Abdoul – Abs duel

Omar – O in the mar (Spanish for sea)

Issouf – Is off?

Aboubacar – A boob in the car

Félix – Felix the Cat

Alain – A lane

Innocent – Innocent

Stephane – Step on knee

Amadou – I'm mad at you

Dieudonne – D done

Issa – Is a?

Victor – Vick's cough drop tore

Aziz – A sneeze

Alexandre – Owl sander

Bernard – Burn yard

Wilfried – Will fried

Jacques – Jacks

Jules – Jewels

Michel – Microphone yell

Peter – Peter Rabbit

Ulrich – Old wrench

Rachid – Ratchet

Pierre – Pier

Justin – Just tan

Ben – Bend

Boris – Board with an S

Arsene – R send

Simon – Simon Memory Game

Frank – Frankfurter

Thierry – There read

Yannick – Yawn

Augustin – A gusting wind

Jonathan – Toilet (John) that's thin

Yacouba – Your scuba

Lamine – La mean (person)

Hamza – Ham saw

Alfred – Owl fried

Claude – Cloud

Daouda – Dowel dot

Frederic – Fried ear

Florent – Florescent

Lionel – Lionel train

laurent – Low rent

Prosper – Press pear

Vincent – Fences

Marcel – Sea (mar is Spanish for sea) in cell

Armel – Arm shaped like L

Desire – Desire her

Jacob – Jacob's ladder

Top 100 East Asian Female Names

Kim – Swim

Lee – Leaves

Park – Park (car)

Minji – Mint G

Yang – Yank

Chen – Chin

Choi – Coy (shy, hiding)

Lily – Lily (flower)

Jane – Chain

Jenny – Chin on knee

Alice – Lice

Wang – Rain

Yujin – Your Gin

Jiwon – You won

Jin – Gin

Amy – Aiming (bull's eye)

Min – Mint

Jeong – Jeans long

Cindy – Cinnamon candy

Lin – Lint

Emily – Hem (pants) with leaves

Li – Leaf

Jieun – Jean un(der)

Han – hand

Jessica – Chest of drawers

Zhang – Drink Tang (drink) then

sleep Zzzz

Anna – Ants on an A

Sujin – Sew Gin

Kang – Tang with a K

Grace – Prayer (grace)

Jung – Chunk

Liu – Lose

Subin – Soup in

Sunny – Sun

Lucy – Loosen

Rachel – Ray on shell

Sarah – Sahara desert

Sumin – Sue man

Yoon – Moon with a Y

Crystal – Crystal ball

Ji Eun – G on

Vivian – Vivid

Ann – Ant

Jisu – G soup

Eunji – Young G

Yu – You

Song – Sing song

Tina – Tea nut

Zoe – Sewing

Cherry – Cherry

Sherry – Bottle of sherry

Jang – Tang with a J

Daisy – Daisy (flower)

Yuri – You read

Ji Young – G young

Bella – Bell with A

Angela – Angel with A

Linda – Window (winda)

Michelle – Missile)

Chloe – Closing

Helen – Mt St Helen's

Jimin – Jamming

Yejin – Yeast gin (drink)

Nicole – Nickels

Huang – Hang

So Yeon – Sew and yawn

Jiyeon – Jean on

Emma – MMA fight

Jo – Cup of Joe (coffee)

Annie – Orphan Annie

Hana – Hand an A

Lisa – Mona Lisa

Sun – Sun

Lim – Limb

Wendy – Windy

Ji Hyun – Jeans (pants) won

Hyewon – Hi to someone who won

Ji Won – She won

Minju – Mint chew

Shin – Shin

Kelly – Key

Yun – U on

Jihye – Jean (pants) heat

Seo – See an O

Claire – Clear

Stella – Steal an A

Min Ji – Mint G

Soyeon – Soy beans on

Sally – Salad

Julia – Jewel in air (for ia)

Kwon – Koala won

Ai – Eye

Hyejin – Hi to Gin (drink)

Irene – Eye ring

Amanda – Man with doves

Sophia – Soak feet

Hannah – Hand an A

Joyce – Joy (happy) ice

Tiffany – Tiffany lamp

Yu Jin – Your chin

Top 100 East Asian Male Names

Kim – Swim

Lee – Leaves

Park – Park (car)

Choi – Coy (shy, hiding)

Chen – Chin

Wang – Tang with a W

Yang – Yank

Zhang – Tang (drink) then sleep Zzzz

Kevin – Cave in

Jason – Jay bird flying to sun

Liu – Leaf ewwww

Jack – Car jack

Li – Leaves

David – Divot

Alex – Owl that licks

John – Toilet

Song – Sing a song

Andy – Ants drinking tea

Eric – Earache

Daniel – Van yell

Shin – Shin

Han – Hand

Lim – Limb

James – Chains

Kang – Tang (drink) with a K

Jang – Change

Lin – Lint

Tom – Tom cat

Peter – Peter Rabbit

Cho – Choke

Yu – You

Jeong – Jeans long

Jin – Gin

Jun – June bug

Tony – Toe and knee

Hong – Bank a gong

Leo – Lion

Jung – Junk

Huang – Hang

Henry – Hen reading

Wu – On roller coaster 'Wooooooooo'

Jay – Blue jay

Zhou – Zoo

Justin – Just in

Chan – Chant

Jerry – Cherry

Chris – Cross

Jo – Cup of Joe (coffee)

Harry – Hairy

Kwon – Koala won

Sean – Yawn

Min – Mind

Oh – O

Michael – Microphone yell

Sam – Uncle Sam

Ryan – Ray gun

Xu – Sue

Zhao – Zoo out (animals escaped)

Nick – Nick (cut)

Seo – See old

Hwang – Hang with W around neck

William – Will and yams

Joe – Cup of Joe (coffee)

Frank – Frankfurter (hot dog)

Mark – Marker

Andrew – Ants that drew

Charles – Charcoal

Steven – Stove on

Sun – Sun

Kasun – Case inside is sun

Jeff – Chef

Yoon – Moon with a Y

Ben – Bend

Yun – You in

Allen – Allen wrench

Brian – Brain

Rahul – Ray in hall

Àî – Eye

Mike – Microphone

Jeon – Jean on

Ken – Ken doll

Edward – Head warden

Bruce – Bruise

Chang – Change

Bob – Bobber (floater when fishing)

Son – Sun

Tharindu – There under

Young – Baby

Joseph – Siphoning cup of Joe (coffee)

An – Ants

Alan – Allen wrench

Ian – E on

Tim – Tin can

Hyun – One

Hu – Who?

Supun – Soup on

Louis – Loose S

Jim – Gym

Paul – Ball

Jiang – Jeans with change (coins)

Top 100 East European Female Names

Anna – Ants on A

Maria – Marry air

Anastasia – Anesthesia

Julia – Jewel in air

Nastya – Nasty

Kate – Kite

Dasha – Dash

Karolina – Caroling

Olga – Old goat

Alina – A leaning

Alexandra – Owl licks sander

Natalia – No towel on ya

Marina – Marina on water

Victoria – Victory

Monika – Harmonica

Marta – Toe in mar (Spanish for sea)

Irina – Eye ring shaped like A

Kasia – Case of air

Ola – Ole!

Aleksandra – Owl licks sander

Liza – Lies down

Mary – Marry

Paulina – Ball lean

Daria – Daring

Elena – A lane

Dominika – Dominican Republic

Diana – Dying ants on an A

Veronika – Fur on a coat

Tanya – Tan ya body

Katya – Cat yarn

Polina – Pole leaning

Ann – Ant

Klaudia – Clouds

Joanna – Show hands

Natasha – No toss

Tereza – Tree saw

Laura – Lower an A

Magda – Mag wheel

Kinga – King's crown letter A around it

Katerina – Cat in arena

Kristina – Christening an A

Yana – Yawn

Ksenia – Kiss knee

Lena – Lean on A

Helen – Mt St Helens

Sofia – Soak feet

Eva – Evening (sunset)

Masha – Mashing

Martina – Martini

Ania – A knee

Irene – Eye ring	Dora – Door
Arina – Arena	Nina – Columbus ship Nina
Ana – Ants on A	Tatiana – Tattoo on ya
Lera – Lead rat	Jana – Tan ya
Martyna – Martini	Kseniya – Kiss knee of yarn
Magdalena – Mag wheel on a doll	Agata – A gator
Agnieszka – Add knees ski	Eszter – A star
Ekaterina – Eating cat in arena	Adéla – A Dell computer
Barbora – Barbed wire	Lucie – Loose E
Andrea – Hand dryer	Yulia – Mule in air
Petra – Rock	Alice – Lice
Christina – Christening an A	Catherine – Cat and hen
Sophie – Soak feet	Oksana – Socks on ya
Viktoria – Victory	Justyna – Just in ya
Michaela – Microphone yell	Valeria – Bowl of leaves
Sasha – Sash	Sara – Say 'Ra'
Barbara – Barbed wire	Nastia – Nasty eye
Weronika – Fur on a coat	Klara – Clearing
Sveta – Sweater	Patrycja – Pat rice
Denisa – Denist	Vika – V cup
Kamila – Camel kneel	Ewa – E weigh (weigh an E)
Svetlana – Sweat land	Natalie – Gnat on leaves
Reka – Wreck	Angelika – Angel licking
Anastasiya – Anesthesia	Sandra – Sander
Helena – Mt St Helens laying	Ira – Eye rod

Top 100 East European Male Names

Alex – Owl that licks

George – Gorge

Dima – Demon

Nikita – Eating nichols

Daniel – Van yell

Alexander – Owl sander

Vlad – Flat

Adam – Adam's apple

Sasha – Sash

Ivan – Eye van

Martin – Martian

David – Divot

Artem – Art with M on it

Peter – Peter rabbit

Anton – Ants on

Sergey – Surging

Mateusz – Door mat oozing

Andrey – Ants reading

Dmitry – DIming tree

Max – Axe

Pavel – Paved L

Jakub – Jacob's ladder

Michael – Microphone yell

Andrew – Ants drew

Bartek – Bar tack

John – Toilet

Roman – Colosseum in Rome

Szymon – Simon memory game

Nick – Nick (cut)

Vladimir – Fat ear

Adrian – A drain

Micha³ – Formica

Patryk – St Patrick

Igor – E gore

Denis – Denist

Kamil – Camel

Andrei – On dryer

Oleg – Old leg

Filip – Philip's screwdriver

Alexandr – Al sander

Vadim – Fat M

Marcin – Cinnamon sea (Spanish for sea is mar)

Dominik – Dominoes

Kirill – High reel

Egor – E gore

Maxim – Axe in

Vladislav – Fat saliva

Michal – Microphone yell

Mark – Marker

Ruslan – Rust land

Jan – Tan

Patrik – St Patrick

Robert – Robot

Ilya – Ill on ya

Paul – Ball

Kuba – Cuban cigar

Kostya – Price tag (cost ya)

Dawid – Da weed

Marek – K in the sea (spanish for mar)

Lukas – Luke Skywalker with S on chest

Sebastian – Sit on bass

Mike – Microphone

Tamás – Thermos

Bogdan – Bog down

Artur – Author

Wojtek – Wash a tack

Maciej – Mace a J

Danil – Van yell

Kostas – Price

Balázs – Applause

Tomas – Thermos

Tasos – Tacos

Alexey – Owl licking an A

Matthew – Door mat words WHO

Vova – Vulva

Tomek – Vomit

Zhenya – Zen (yoga)

Karol – A roll

Krystian – Kissing a ton

Petr – Peter rabbit

Tom – Tom cat

László – Last slow

Bálint – Ball lint

Stelios – Steeling Os

Tomáš – Thermos

Wiktor – VIc cough drops tearing

Damian – Da man

István – Is the van?

Manos – Minnows

Ondøej – On dojo

Roland – Rolling ants

Ákos – Acres

Yaroslav – Yeah row in saliva

Konstantinos – Constantly standing on toes

Honza – Phone saw

Gleb – Green lip

Chris – Cross

Daniil – Van yell

Boris – Board with S

Kacper – Casper the ghost

Top 100 South American Female Names

Camila – Camel with vanilla

Gabriela – Angel Gabriel with an A

Maria – Sea eating (mar = sea)

Daniela – Van yelling at an A

Laura – Lowering an A

Natalia – Gnats in leaves (in air for ia)

Mariana – Marrying ants

Andrea – On dryer

Ana – Ants on nuts

Fernanda – Fern (plant) handing

Sofia – Soak feet

Julia – Jewel in air

Amanda – A man with doves

Jessica – Chest of drawers

Paula – Ball with an A

Beatriz – Bee in trees

Juliana – Jewelry with ants

Leticia – Lettuce

Victória – Victory

Carolina – A roll in a line of A's

Agustina – A gusting wind eating

Larissa – La wrist

Thais – Thaw ice

Rocío – Row sit and say O

Sara – Sahara desert

Vitoria – V that's being torn

Luana – Lousiana

Alejandra – A hand dryer

Rafaela – Rough an L & A

Karen – Carrot

Carla – Car lost

Bruna – Brunette

Lorena – Low rain on an A

Valentina – Valentine card

Verônica – Fur harmonica

Isabela – Is a bell

Angie – Ants drinking tea

Barbara – Barbed wire

Francisca – France with Sister

Paola – Ball with an A

Aline – A line

Diana – Dying ants on an A

Cristina – Christening an A

Brenda – Bent window (winda)

Stephanie – Step on knees

Romina – Roaming

Gaby – Talking a lot

Florencia – Floor rent

Tatiana – Tatto

Adriana – A drain on ya

Anna – Ants on an A

Raquel – Rock L

Luisa – Look east

Lívia – Living

Marcela – Sea (mar = sea) in a cell

Catalina – Cat leaning

Micaela – Microphone yell

Lucia – Loosen

Luciana – Losing an ant

Sabrina – Submarine

Angelica – Angel licking

Nathalia – Gnat on owl

Clara – Clearing

Caroline – A roll in a line

Helena – Mt St Helen's

Valéria – Ballerina

Nicole – Nickels

Yessica – Yes I can!

Tamara – Tamborene

Andressa – Ants on dresser

Ana Clara – Ants in clearing

Lara – Lair (den) of A's

Erika – Earache

Gabrielle – Gabriel the angel

Luiza – Look east see a Z

Giovanna – G on a van

Constanza – Con(vict) standing

Maria Clara – Sea eating (mar) a clearing

Vanessa – Van full of S's

Patricia – Pat rice in air

Sarah – Sahara desert

Belén – Bell in

Mary – Married

Mayra – Saying, 'My Ra!'

Evelyn – Violin

Ana Maria – Ants in sea eating(mar= sea)

Raissa – Racing

Gabriella – Gabriel the angel with an A

Milena – Mile of N's

María José – Sea (mar) in air with hose

Abril – A pill

Aléxia – A licks in air

Nadia – Nadar (to swim in Spanish)

Taynara – Tape an R on

Yasmin – Yes man

Emilia – A meal in air (for ia)

Paulina – Ball in an line

Michele – Missile

Sandra – Sander

Melisa – Molasses

Top 100 South American Male Names

Lucas – Luke Skywalker with S on chest

Gabriel – Gabriel the angel

Daniel – Van yell

Juan – One

Matheus – Door mat hue

Diego – Day go

Pedro – Pay for rope

Santiago – Sand tea go

Leonardo – Lean in a yard of O's

Felipe – Fill leap

Carlos – Car lost

Andres – San Andres fault

João – Jaw

David – Divot

Vinicius – Finish us

José – Wate hose

Guilherme – Gill hurt me

Luiz – Low wheeze

Sebastian – Sit on bass

Rafael – Rough an L

Marcos – Mark us

Paulo – Ball of O's

Bruno – Bruise nose

Luis – Loose S

Victor – Vic's Cough drop tore

Gustavo – Gust of O's

Pablo – Pop low

Fernando – Fern (plant) ants

Thiago – Tea that goes

Leandro – Leaves ants draw

Rodrigo – Rod read go

Mateus – Mat hay us

Camilo – Chameleon

Ricardo – Brick card O

Nicolás – Nichols

Cristian – Christian cross

Alejandro – Owl hand throw

Joao Pedro – Jaw pay for rope

Arthur – Author

Eduardo – Head ward of O's

Anderson – Ants in the sun

Vitor – V tore

Igor – E gore

Franco – Frankfurter shaped like O

Douglas – Dig glass

Caio – Cow

Matias – My tie us

Francisco – San Francisco Golden Gate Bridge

Jhon – Toilet

Sergio – Surging O's	Emanuel – Email
Miguel – My gill	Alexis – Lexus car
Willian – Will in	Juan Carlos – One car lost
Jorge – Whore in the hay	Richard – Wrench in yard
Alex – Owl licks	Raul – Roll
Joaquín – Walking	Federico – Fed a reading coat
Henrique – Hen reading a K	Renan – Raining
Julian – Jewelry in	Erick – E brick
Fábio – Fatty O	Tomás – Thermos
Alexandre – Owl licks sander	Raphael – Rough an L
Jonathan – Thin toilet (John)	Alan – Allen wrench
Mauricio – More ice	Facundo – Fact under
Luciano – Loose on you	Walter – Wall tear
Ivan – Eye van	Italo – Towel O
Jesus – Jesus	Josue – Hoe sway
Fabricio – Fabric of O's	Jaime – Hi May!
Kevin – Cave in	Christian – Christian cross
Andre – Andre the Giant	William – Will and yams
Augusto – A gust of O's	Marcelo – Mar (sea in Spanish) of Jell-O
Agustin – A gusting	Henry – Hen reading
Javier – Has air	Maicon – Making Bacon
Thomas – Thermos	Hernan – Hurt hand
Alexander – Owl licks sander	Jefferson – Chef in the sun
Joao Vitor – Jaw V tore	Manuel – Manual
Michael – Microphone yell	Ezequiel – Easy kill
Flavio – Flying V and O	

Top 100 West Asian Female Names

Merve – Nerve

Zeynep – Zzzzz nap

Elif – Elf

Büþra – Boob red

Gizem – Karate Gi seam

Beyza – Bay Sleeping Zzzzz

Esra – S run

Irem – Eye cream

Ezgi – A ski

Ceren – Siren

Gamze – Games

Ece – Ice

Kübra – Cobra

Buse – Bus

Selin – Ceiling

Burcu – Bear cub

Hilal – Hill owl

Betül – Bed tool

Özge – Wizard of OZ Geee

Deniz – Dentist

Eda – Eat A

Sena – See no

Fatma – Fat mom

Damla – Dam load

Ecem – Cement

Melis – Melons

Melike – Me like (smiley face)

Rabia – Rabbit

Ýrem – Rim (wheel)

Nur – Nerd

Busra – Bus run

Ebru – A brew

Hatice – Hat of ice

Duygu – Day goo

Dilara – Deal R's

özlem – Muslim

Aype – Ape

Ceyda – Cedar

Ilayda – Lay down

Þeyma – Payment

Emine – Mine for E's

Cansu – Can soup

Yaren – Yard rent

Tuðçe – Two cakes

Seda – Set A

Yasemin – Yes man

Zehra – Zebra

Yaðmur – Yah in mirror

Pelin – Pile in

Sude – Suit

Melisa – Molasses

Aslý – Ash leaves

Hazal – Hazel nut	Melek – Me lick
Sinem – Signing	Serra – Sahara desert
Ayse – Line of A's	Rumeysa – Rum (drink) in eye
Sýla – Seal up	Ayþenur – Ape in air
Derya – Dare ya	Seyma – Say 'ma'
ayça – Aching	Berfin – Bear fin
Begüm – Bee gum	Neslihan – Nestle in hand
Tuba – Tuba	çaðla – Kaola
Tuðba – Tow boat	Su – Sue
Feyza – Face Zzzz (sleep)	Bilge – Builds
Hande – Hand	Seher – See her
Pýnar – Pine tar	Meryem – Marry them
Aleyna – A lane of A's	Sibel – Sigh Bell (Bell sighing)
Sümeyye – Some eye	Edanur – Head in your
Aylin – Ailing	Ayþegül – Ape in (sea)gull
Selen – Selling	Ozge – Wizard of OZ Geee
Bahar – Bee hair	Dilek – Dill pickle lick
Eylül – Aisle	Gökçe – Goat see
Nisa – Knees on	Gözde – Ghost tea
Dilan – Dealing	Beste – Best friends
Öykü – Boy coo	Esma – Is my
Zeliha – Sell hay	Yagmur – Yank mirror
Beril – Barrel	Tugba – Tug boat
Ekin – Elk	Rana – Ran

Top 100 West Asian Male Names

Mehmet – My mitt

Burak – Brr rock

Emre – M read

Ali – All leaves

Ahmet – A mitt

Mustafa – Mustard off

Furkan – Fur can

Mert – Merge

Murat – Moo rat

Fatih – Fatty

Can – Can

Onur – On your

Enes – E niece

Deniz – Denist

Hasan – Has on

Kaan – Con man

Eren – E rent

Ibrahim – E bra on him

Hakan – Hack on

Kadir – Cut ear

Osman – O's man (letter O)

Alperen – Owl pairing

Yusuf – Yourself

Muhammed – Muhammed Ali

Umut – U mutt (dog)

Yavuz – Ya lose

Yiðit – Hit it

Alper – Owl pepper

Samet – Uncle Sam met

Arda – Art with an A

Kerem – Carom shot in billards

Ömer – O on a mare

Berkay – Brrrr K

Yasin – Yea! cinnamon

Kemal – Key to mall

Batuhan – Bat in your hand

Kayra – K run

Yunus – You nose

Ege – Edge

Barýþ – Bar up

Serhat – Sir hat

Ismail – Is mail?

Görkem – Gore cam(era)

Mohammad – Mohammad Ali

Hüseyin – Owl (who) saying

Berke – Brr kitty

Volkan – Volt can

Semih – Semi truck

Serdar – Saw there

Erkan – Ear can

Ozan – O sand

Baran – Bee ran

Serkan – Sir can	Doðukan – Doe in a can
Cem – Sim card	Halil – Hall ill
Taha – Tahoe	Alp – Alps
Oguzhan – Goo in hand	Anil – A kneel
Ahmed – Ahh mad!	Omer – Homer
Okan – Old can	Ýbrahim – E bra on him
Sefa – See feet	Oðuz – O deuce
Efe – F hay	Bora – Boring
Selim – Ceiling	Cihan – See hand
Harun – Hair run	Emrah – M run
Erhan – Ear hand	Metin – meeting
Sinan – Send ant	özgür – O that's curved
Berk – Burnt	Ramazan – Ram a van
Gökhan – Goat hand	Yigit – You get
Abdullah – Abs dueling	Kenan – Key nun
Ufuk – Oooo foot	Mete – Met A
Bilal – Bill all	ömer faruk – Homer far
Ugur – U girl	Sezer – Ceasar
Anýl – A kneel	Fýrat – Fry rat
Salih – Salt hill	Utku – Youth cut
Oðuzhan – O deuce hand	Taner – Tanner (very tan)
Talha – Tall haha	Ben – Bend
Zafer – Safer	Hamza – Ham saw
Tolga – Toll goat	Muhammad – Muhammed Ali

Free $27 Name memory training videos gift.
Get it at memorizenames.com

TRIPLE Your Memory TRIPLE Your Business

FUN meeting!

EXCITING!

AMAZING!

This is the most comprehensive memory training seminar on the market today. Ron White is not only a memory trainer and a U.S.A. Memory Champion, but is also a business owner and entrepreneur. He understands what it takes to keep a business successful. His seminar isn't about teaching you how to memorize your grocery list — he teaches you how to use your memory to maximize profits and production in a business!!

In this 1-day, 6-hour memory training class your group will learn:

- How to build relationships by remembering names and faces
- How to build confidence by giving speeches without notes
- Save money and time because you don't have to retrain your staff (they
- remember it the first time)
- Increase your knowledge of any subject in 1/3 the time
- Become a subject matter expert on any topic

This is a Vegas Show with Harvard level education. Ron will memorize up to 300 names in the audience and then a 50 digit number right in front of your eyes and then repeat from memory to the amazement and entertainment of your group!

Can be done as a 1-hour keynote at your conference or up to 6-hour training.

Ron White is a two-time U.S.A. Memory Champion, has held the record for fastest to memorize a deck of cards in the U.S.A. and has been a guest on *Good Morning America, Fox News, Martha Stewart, Dr. Oz,* History Channel, Discovery Channel, National Geographic Channel, *ABC World News,* the *Today Show* and many other programs. A University of Texas scientist on the History Channel show *Superhumans* determined that Ron uses 35% more of his brain than the average person when he memorizes. **What would a 35% increase in brain power mean for your business?**

Email ron@ronwhitetraining.com
with subject line:
Memory keynote/workshop

Ron White U.S.A. MEMORY CHAMPION & MEMORY RECORD HOLDER

To book this valuable workshop, contact Ron at 972-801-5330.

Printed in Great Britain
by Amazon

13974936R00056